Insanity Streak

Book 3

GW00363529

TONY LOPES

ℛℛ
RAVETTE PUBLISHING

This edition first published by Ravette Publishing 2006.

Printed and bound in Malta for
Ravette Publishing Limited
Unit 3, Tristar Centre
Star Road, Partridge Green
West Sussex RH13 8RA

ISBN 10: 1-84161-266-9
ISBN 13: 978-1-84161-266-9

Foreword

How do you know a good cartoon when you see it?
What kind of humour will apply right across the range
of a five million readership?

The sources of laughter are notoriously diverse,
the effects of a particular joke famously subjective.
With responsibility for the Daily Mail's regular daily cartoon strips,
I receive as many as three new submissions a week - all worth a look
... some worth thinking seriously about.

When Tony's first cartoons arrived,
I saw immediately that it was a new classic.

Andy Simpson - Daily Mail, UK

Primitive Toothpicks

AND DAVID, DO YOU PROMISE TO FOLLOW LUISA AROUND SHOPPING AND NOT GET BORED?

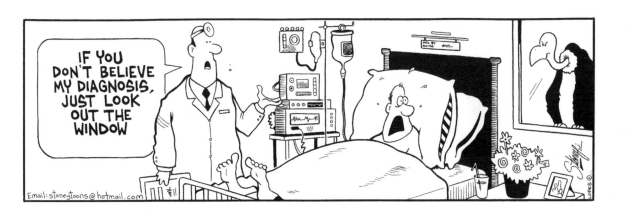

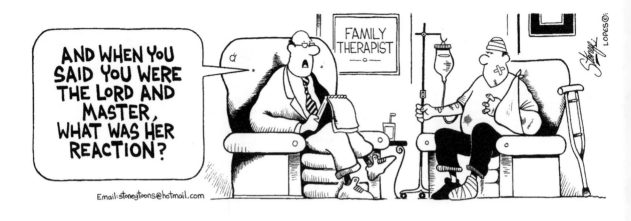

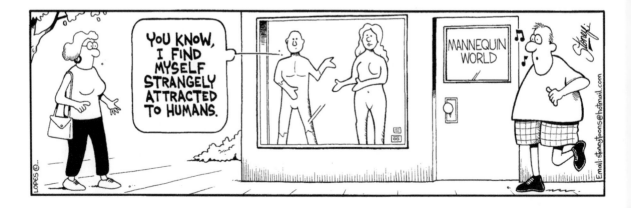